The Dream State

The fourth poetic collection

by

Esperanza Habla

© 2018 La Luna Press, L.L.C.

ISBN: 978-1-7322188-0-2

Library of Congress Control Number: 2018945389

Cover design and all photographs by Esperanza Habla
Author portrait courtesy of Kristen Pugh Photography
Logo for La Luna Press by Adam Whitaker

Cover Photography: ©Kristina McKune
Great Basin National Park, Nevada
Taken on a Canon 5D MarkIII

Contributor: ©Kristina McKune
Written and photographic work contributed with permission
of artist. © All rights reserved.

For permission requests, write to the publisher, at the address
below.

La Luna Press, L.L.C.
P.O. Box 533284
Indianapolis, IN
46253
USA

Thank you for purchasing
this book.

For more information,
please visit us at:

www.lalunapress.com

La Luna Press

Thank you to my dear family for their never-ending love and support.

Thank you to you, the reader.

Thank you for reading this book.

To the blog readers.

Thank you for reading my

letters to the moon.

Table of Contents:

Table of Contents continued:

Every Single Sound   October 4, 2013

I am at work with a splitting headache. I believe it is a
migraine. If you have ever had a migraine, you know what
I am feeling right now. If you have never had a migraine, they
are hard to describe.

Migraines are severe headaches which cause different
symptoms in different people. Some people see colored lights
in front of their eyes. Some people are sensitive to sounds.
Some people get physically sick from a migraine. Some take
medicine and are feeling better in a manner of hours. Some
suffer for days.

Some can function, some cannot. It just depends on the
person, and the cause and severity of the headache. For me,
when I have a true migraine, I am sensitive to sights and
sounds. I usually take some medicine, lie down in a dark room,
and do everything I can to not be physically ill. I am thankful
that I do not have a migraine often.

My headache began yesterday. There was a screaming baby in
my library. Her mother was preoccupied on a computer. The
baby was, as all babies are, impatient, and craved its mother's
attention. The mother was oblivious to her child screaming.
After an hour, I noticed I had a headache. I went to my purse
and took some medicine.

In the afternoon, my headache was getting better. Until it was
time to go home. The day began rainy and overcast, not a ray
of sunshine. The day finished with sunny blue skies. I broke
one of my life lessons, one of my cardinal rules: "Never go
anywhere without your sunglasses."

The Dream State

There I was, in my car, with a twenty minute drive in front of me, in rush hour traffic, with bright sunny skies, and no sunglasses. I squinted my way home. Today I noticed I was feeling better, but I still had my headache. Then, after the library opened, I noticed the sounds.

People think that libraries are quiet, academic places of study. That image is archaic and could not be farther from the truth. Libraries are now gathering places for communities. Instead of being quiet as tombs, libraries are vibrant places, alive with the rich sounds of people as they gather as a community and search for knowledge in a variety of formats and sources.

Today, after the library opened, I noticed the sounds. I have noticed every sound in this building. Thankfully, it is not a busy day; however, when you have a very bad headache, sounds are often magnified. For some, sounds can be an annoyance; for others, sounds can be like an icepick to the head.

When I was on my lunch break, the sounds became too much. I did the best thing I knew to do; I pulled out my mp3 player, my ear buds, and played some soft, very soothing music. To many, it would seem counterintuitive for me to do so, to listen to music when sounds are bothering me. However, it was just what I needed at the time.

I was transported to a quiet, peaceful space. For those twenty minutes or so, I was able to drown out the sounds of the world and get some peace.

Imagine it for a moment. You are in a public place with a bad headache. Your eyes hurt. Your head hurts. You begin to notice every single sound.

The automated voice from the computer.
A screaming baby. People talking on cell phones. Computer keys clacking. Plastic cases opening and closing. The telephone ringing. A paper cutter squeaking. People talking. Children's feet running on carpet. The lawnmower out back. A co-worker talking. A co-worker listening to opera on YouTube.
The opening and closing of doors.
Food in your mouth as you chew it. Ice cubes clinking in drinks. Keys jingling. Cell phones ringing. The automatic door opening and closing. The carnival type music on the computers for children. The whir of the copy machine. Cars accelerating on the street. Cabinets opening and closing. The sound of the hand dryer in the bathroom.

Every single sound.

This is my world today. This is where I am right now. I do not have a full-blown migraine; if I did, I would not be able to function.

I have had many full-on migraines in the past, and I know there is a difference between that and what I am experiencing now.

I wish I were at home on my couch, sleeping away the migraine.

But I cannot go home. I have a job to do. I am here, serving the public, trying not to let my headache ruin my day-or anyone else's day.

Sensitive to every single sound.

Generosity   October 10, 2013

What do you think of when you hear the word "generosity?" Generosity is defined as "the act of giving without expecting anything in return." Generosity is a sister to kindness, thoughtfulness, benevolence, consideration.

Generosity is an attribute that is seldom found these days. We all have the potential to be generous. I know within my heart that, when I am generous with someone, that generosity will return to me.

In my short career as a writer, I have been blessed to meet many types of artists from around the world. Their generosity has been overwhelming. These artist friends have also been instrumental in helping me research my book. I have queried my artist friends many times; every time I asked, I received an answer within minutes. I am thankful to each and every one of them. I would not be where I am today without their help and generosity.

I feel that as artists, we should be generous with one another. As people, we should be generous with one another.

As many people have been generous to me, it is now my turn to be helpful to others. I will shortly begin a new project on this blog; I will be featuring people that have begun new creative endeavors. Right now I have two people slated to appear. Both individuals are artists, successful in their careers.

These artists will be appearing in the coming days. Watch this space.

Candidly   October 12, 2013

It is a wondrous thing, to find an artist whose work speaks to
you. I would like to introduce you to such an artist. Her name
is Kristina McKune. Kristina is a photographer and a true
master in her craft. I have been a fan of her work for years. She
is a prolific artist whose work is highly collectible. I am
fortunate in that I own two of her pieces. Her work is
unparalleled. Come see for yourself. Ladies and gentlemen,
I present the guest artist for today, Kristina McKune.............

Photographs bring me pure, absolute joy. Seeing the world captured
in still imagery has always been a way for me to process and
understand it better. I am moved by what other artists choose to
capture and share. I am awed by the way photography can raise
awareness about global concerns & motivate us to help in whatever
way we can. And I love how none of us can escape the flood of
memory & emotion when we look at personal snapshots from our
own collections.

It's the act of taking the photograph, though, which affects me the
deepest. Capturing a person, a moment, a place in a way I feel does
justice is one of the most gratifying experiences I am lucky enough
to have on a semi-regular basis. Being able to hold an image I have
taken and show another person my point of view allows me to truly
connect with those around me and with the world at large.

Iceland, 2012 © Kristina McKune

I received my Bachelor of Fine Arts Degree with a concentration in photography from Towson University in 2005. I put my art on hold for years and have only recently allowed myself to pursue it as a full time career. Since relocating to Denver, Colorado I have opened a shop on Etsy where my photographic prints are for sale. I also have launched a line of greeting cards featuring my original photography. Being a small business owner as well as an artist, I am constantly adapting to new demands and learning as I go. The rewards are as numerous as the challenges! I feel incredibly lucky to be doing something I am so passionate about. When you really love what you do, it doesn't feel like work at all.

Field of Dreams site, 2012 © Kristina McKune

Find me here:

    Blog: https://kristinamarshae.tumblr.com
    E-mail: kristina@candidly.org

Thank you, Esperanza, for sharing your space with me!

A Person of Faith   October 15, 2013

The topic of religion has come up many times in my online friendships. Many friends have assumed I shared their religion; many assumed I was another. Some online friends have sent me religious photos; some have asked me my opinion of the bible.

When my online friends send me religious photos, I thank them for sending them to me. They do not know that I do not share their religious beliefs; it is easier to thank someone for sending a photo than offending someone by asking why they sent me such an image.

There is a saying in my country-
"Don't talk about religion or politics between friends."

However, I feel that I need to talk about religion, and faith, so that everyone will understand my point of view.

To talk about religion, one must first examine the different faiths of the world. I am in the category of Christians. I grew up in a Protestant religion called Presbyterian. I have two family members who are ministers in the Presbyterian Church.

I grew up in the church, living the life of a dutiful parishioner. I didn't question why or how, I just believed. As I grew older, I began to ask questions of why and how, what I believed and why. Like many young parishioners, I left the church.

I am a religious person. I am a person of faith. I do not have a definition for my religious point of view. Organized religion does not work for me. I am a Christian; other than that, I do not subscribe to a title of religion.

If you do not subscribe to a title of religion, what do you believe? I believe that the Bible is a collection of stories, told by men, passed down through the millennia. I believe that there is a higher power, which I refer to as God. I believe in God. I pray to God every night. I do not go to church.

How can you say you are a Christian when you do not go to church? I practice my faith every day, in my actions towards others. I practice my faith every night, in prayer to God. I do not need to go to a church to pray, nor to connect with God. As I told a friend once:

> **"Just because I don't go to God's house every week doesn't mean I don't know where he lives."**

I believe in heaven. I do not believe in hell. I believe in God. I do not believe in a devil. I believe in the Golden Rule, which states to treat others as you would want to be treated. I believe in doing good deeds for others. I believe that the good of those deeds will come back to me. I believe that, regardless of what religion we are, what religious beliefs we hold dear, or even if we have no religious beliefs at all, we are more alike than we are different. I believe we are all here for a common purpose- to find our purpose in life, and to use that purpose to help as many people as we can.

We are all here for a reason. God does not make mistakes.

The Perfect Fit   September 28, 2013

On a recent shopping excursion, I had a difficult time trying to find something that fit me.

I picked out several blouses in my size to try on. I knew my size, and knew I would not have trouble with these selections. I was wrong. The size I knew was not correct. I was the next size up.

I then began a tirade of negative thinking. Amidst my defeat, I decided to try on another shirt. To my astonishment, it fit! I stood there confused; I was the same body size, yet both of the shirts, which were same size, did not fit. What was the explanation?

The answer was simple-sizes. The two blouses were not the same size. They had the same letter on the label, yet they were not the same size. There is no consistency in sizes of clothing. Sizes vary due to the fabric of the blouse, the design and cut. I knew that sizes varied between labels; I had no idea they varied within the same label.

In a recent commercial, a social experiment took place. Women went in to a store to try on jeans. When the ladies went to look for a size of jeans, they did not see a number or a letter on a label. The ladies had to get measured to find out their size. Words like "radiant", "charismatic" and "fabulous" were on the tape measure-not numbers.

Judging by the looks of the women's faces in the commercial, they were elated. They were in jeans that fit their bodies, and were not defined by a number or a letter. They were defined by a wonderful word instead. The women were radiant, charismatic, and fabulous.

That day in that store, I did exactly what those women did. I threw out all the rules. I decided to not pay any attention to the little letters on the labels. I looked for blouses that would look good on me, were sized to fit me, that flattered me.

I literally broke the rules when buying those blouses. I bought a shirt with horizontal stripes. I bought a shirt with a beautiful print. I was definitely out of my comfort zone. Yet, I found a new comfort zone-the zone of breaking the rules, of finding what works for me.

So what is the moral of the story? Clothes vary as much as the people trying them on. We come in all different colors, all different shapes and sizes.

If you find yourself shopping for clothes and need to go a size up, do not attack yourself. It's not you, it's the clothes. Sizes vary by style and label.

Be willing to expand your horizon, to break the rules we have been indoctrinated with, to be courageous enough to think outside the box.

Above all, do not define yourself by a number on a scale or by a letter on a label.

Find what works for you. Find the perfect fit.

The Nightmare   October 24, 2013

I have not had a nightmare in quite some time. Last night
I had a nightmare. Or maybe it was early this morning.
In the nightmare, I was watching a movie. No, I wasn't just
watching the scenes, I was in them. Random scenes of gun
violence flashed before me. I saw people getting shot. I saw
people shooting.

I then saw Robert Kennedy and John F. Kennedy sitting in the
Oval Office in the White House. Both of them were shot and
killed. Robert was on a couch; John was in a chair. They talked
to one other. They were bloody. Their clothes, their skin,
bloody. They had no knowledge of nor paid any attention to
their present state. They just kept talking to each other. Again
and again and again I saw images of shooting, killing. I then
heard a voice.....

> **"You live in a country where a man
> can shoot another man and not go to prison."**

I then saw a face from a famous, criminal murder case. Case in
point. Again I saw killing. I saw people aiming guns at other
people, shooting, killing.

I awoke with a gasp. I sat up in bed, my heart pounding.
Why would I have dreamt that you might ask? It's simple-
because gun violence is everywhere. We in the U.S. are almost
becoming complacent. We hear of a shooting on the news, and
do not think anything of it. Shootings appear to be
commonplace.

In December of 2012, a gunman in the state of Connecticut
went into a school and shot 20 children and 6 adults. The
country was outraged. The country fell to its knees with grief.
The country mourned. The world mourned with us. We swore

nothing like that would ever happen again. Yet in the U.S., nothing has been done to stop the killing. Nothing.

This year, in the U.S., there have been 12 mass killings from gun violence. Two more shootings took place in schools in the United States this week. The first of these shootings involved a student with a gun, and a teacher who jumped in front of the gun to spare others from hurt. The teacher died from his injuries. The other shooting involved one teacher and one student; the student shot and killed the teacher. They found the teacher's body on the grounds of the school.

Last week, in my city, there were three killings from gun violence in one night. The shootings took place within twenty minutes. Three deaths. Within twenty minutes.

I am in favor of people owning guns for means of self-protection and for hunting, to provide food for their family. I am not in favor of people having access to military weapons who are not in the military. You can hunt for food and protect your family without an automatic rifle.

We need to have serious discussions in this country, about background checks, mental health, and many other issues. This phenomenon was not created overnight; it will not be solved overnight.

Haven't enough people died from the violence? What will it take? Something must be done. Enough is enough.

I pray that we find a solution to this problem.

I pray that there will be no further nightmares.

A Life of Abundance   October 29, 2013

I recently saw a post online that urged the reader to ask for what you want. Asking your friends, family members, for whatever you want.

The post also talked about asking God-or your version of a higher power- and the universe for what you want. If you want love, ask for it. If you want wealth, ask for it.

If you want a fancy house, ask for it. Ask the Lord and the universe for whatever you want. Ask and ye shall receive, right?

To me, the post made me suspicious. Or maybe dubious is a better word. You can ask for anything under the moon; however, it does not mean that you are going to get it. It is almost like asking Santa Claus for a prized toy. Sometimes Santa Claus brings the toy you asked for; other times he does not.

In the past, I asked friends for what I wanted. I asked my friends detailed, specific things about what I wanted.
I received nothing in return. These friends could not give me what they themselves did not have to give.

The more I thought about the post I had seen, I became intrigued. I had asked friends for what I wanted. But I had never asked God for what I want. I had never asked the universe for what I want. If I were to ask God, the universe, for what I want, what would that be? What would I ask for?

After much thought, I knew what to ask for. In a moment of prayer, I decided to be brave, to take the leap, and ask for what I want. I sat in bed, raised my hands skyward, and asked for what I want....a life of abundance.

The word abundance can be described as to be in possession of a great amount of something; the word abundance can also mean prosperity, fullness and benevolence.

I want an abundant life. I want to be successful as a writer.

I want my publishing business to be successful.

I want to have enough money when I get to my retirement.

I want to live in a house by the ocean.

I want to meet a man, my indigo knight, fall in love with him and share the rest of my life with him.

I want to travel the world. I want to continue to help others as I have been helped.

I have done as I was directed. I asked God and the universe for what I want.

Will I receive what I asked for?

I cannot wait to find out.

Setbacks   November 6, 2013

Have you ever worked for something so hard, tried with all your might to accomplish your goal, to make your dream come true, to then experience a setback? Setbacks, or obstacles or delays in fulfilling our goals and dreams can be very upsetting and challenging.

I recently suffered a setback. A couple of months ago, I began having problems with my home computer. I could not turn the computer on. When I was successful in turning it on, the computer could not run the operating system (the brain of the computer.) Nothing worked as it should; the computer was even running programs I never installed.

After consulting with a person who works on computers, I found that my computer had several trojan horse viruses on it. The viruses lay dormant on the computer, and one day attacked.

I was sent into an absolute panic. The files for my books of poetry are on that computer. Thankfully I was able to save them to an external memory device. I was also able to save some of my photographs from years past. I was relieved to save those photographs; some of the photos were from trips I have taken, others from family gatherings that will never happen again.

As of right now, my computer will not turn on, will not function. It is an expensive paperweight. I have begun to shop for a new computer. I cannot hope to run my publishing company or publish my books without one.

I have a good friend who also suffered a setback recently. My friend is a successful writer and publisher. He recently built a website for a new creative endeavor. He built the website himself, which took him months.

When the website was complete, I asked my friend if he would like me to feature him and his new website here, on this blog. He wrote me back and said that he would like that.

A week or so later I wrote him to see if he was ready to be featured. He wrote me back with upsetting news. His website account had been hacked (or broken into.)

Everything he had painstakingly built was destroyed in a matter of minutes. My friend is now building his website again, piece by piece. I will feature him once the website is up and operational again.

Setbacks are bumps in the road to our end goal, detours in our paths. While they can be devastating, we can also look at them as tests of our strength and perseverance, challenges we must complete before we can proceed.

If we believe in ourselves, our goals, if we are steadfast, we can overcome the setbacks that befall us. Do not let any setback divert you from your path. Persevere. Make your dreams come true.

Dreams Do Come True   November 13, 2013

Hello everyone, I thought I would take a moment and let you know what is going on in my world.

I am still without a computer. I am shopping for a new one. There is a lot to learn about computers in the years since I last bought one. I want to purchase one that I can grow into, one that will help me in my publishing business, one that will last for years to come.

Because I am without a computer, I am only able to write on this blog from a computer at my workplace, on my break time. Also, because I am without a computer, the publication of my books has been delayed.

When I decided to publish books of my poetry myself and start my own publishing company, I originally planned to publish all of my books at once. However, due to this delay, I have decided to publish the books as they are ready.

My first collection of poetry, "I am Hope," is almost ready. I anticipate a January release of this book, in book and electronic book format. The Spanish version of this first collection of poetry will be the next one to be published.

The second collection of my poetry, "The Bigger Picture," will be the next volume published, in English and then Spanish.

Because I have continued to write on this blog, I have material for another collection of poetry. I plan to create my third collection of poetry, "Symphonies."

I used to believe that dreams did not come true. I have seen it happen. Dreams do come true. When my books are finally published, it will be a dream come true for me. I cannot wait for that day.

Life does not always go the way we planned. Sometimes we encounter bumps and turns in the road, and our dreams and goals do not turn out the way we planned. However, maybe that means that our dreams will be bigger, better, and more fulfilling than we ever could have fathomed or imagined.

Thank you for accompanying me on my journey. Thank you for helping make my dream come true.

The Dream State   November 22, 2013

Every night when I go to bed, I settle in and I begin to pray.
                    Lord, I thank you for this day.

I then review the day I have had, the good, the bad, and the ugly. My thoughts then focus on the day to come, and what I will need to accomplish. It is at that point that I begin to drift into sleep, into sub consciousness.

Between sleep and wake, I enter the dream state.

It is in the dream state that I often have my highest level of creativity, receive the most inspiration. Thoughts, ideas, concepts, words, phrases enter my mind, in a whirlwind of activity.

The Dream State

I do not know if my brain has created these things, or if these things have been given to me.

When I wake, I remember some thoughts from the dream state. My usual pattern is to think about them for a few days, try to remember that state, review the thoughts, and wait to see a clearer picture.

Once the thoughts have aligned, I begin to write. If the thoughts do not align on paper, I leave the piece and come back to it later.

Not everything from the dream state is retained. I have written poems, even songs in the dream state, complete with verses and melodies. In the rare times that this happened, in the morning, the poems and songs were gone. I remember that they happened, yet I cannot retain them.

Perhaps those lost thoughts and songs will come back to me, in another dream state. Maybe I should keep a pen and paper by my bedside, to write things down. A dream state journal.

What do I write and share here? Poems? Writings? Blog entries? Perhaps.

However, maybe, more succinctly,
contents of the dream state.

20

Give Thanks   November 28, 2013

Today in my country is the Thanksgiving holiday. Thanksgiving was established by President Abraham Lincoln in 1863, when our nation was in a civil war. The day was established to be on the fourth Thursday in the month of November every year. The purpose of the day is to gather with family and friends, to have a feast together, and to pause and reflect on all that we have, to be thankful for all the blessings we have been given. The feast of Thanksgiving is to remember the feast in the 1600s with the native people in this land and the English settlers in this new land known as America.

I have to say, this is my least favorite holiday. Do not misunderstand me, there are things that I like about this holiday. I love the time to gather with friends and family and to reflect on everything I am thankful for. I love watching the Thanksgiving Parade. I love watching Thanksgiving animated specials. It is not Thanksgiving without animated specials.

However, there are some traditions about Thanksgiving Day that I do not care for. American football for one. Enjoying sports is not in my nature. I watch the Olympics when they occur, yet I do not care for any other sports.

Another tradition I do not care for is shopping on the day after Thanksgiving. This day is known as Black Friday, meaning that it is one of the biggest shopping days for retailers. Personally I think it is called Black Friday because of the behavior exhibited that day. People push and shove one another just to save some money on their purchases. Two years ago, a security guard at a retail store was trampled to death by people entering the store to do their shopping.

It used to be that people would camp out in tents at the stores; they used to open at 5am on Friday morning, and then they opened at midnight, 12am Friday morning. Now the practice has seeped into Thanksgiving Day. Some retail stores are opening at 5pm today. If people are out shopping, the employees at the stores cannot spend holiday time with their family.

The other thing I do not care for is the traditional Thanksgiving feast. Usually the meal has turkey as the entrée, followed by side dishes such as green beans, mashed potatoes, sweet potatoes, dressing, stuffing, cranberry sauce, bread, rolls, and then followed by desserts such as pumpkin pie, pecan pie, and apple pie. One thing that is not generally know about me-yet anyone in my family can tell you-I am a very picky eater. I like two or three of the foods I just mentioned. I do not like most of the foods in the traditional Thanksgiving feast.

I mentioned this fact the other day while at work. One co-worker remarked that they never have the traditional Thanksgiving feast, like the one I just described. Every year they have foods from other nations, such as Italy or Greece. This year they are having a feast of Mexican foods. I complimented her on her brave culinary choices.

Yet, at the same time, another co-worker looked at her in total astonishment. She thought having a meal on Thanksgiving that was not the traditional Thanksgiving feast was sacrilegious, almost as though it made her un-American. It does not matter what you eat on Thanksgiving Day. It does not matter if you gather with friends and family for a mammoth feast. It doesn't matter if you watch football, or the parade on television. There are many ways to celebrate the holiday. The point of the holiday is to pause and reflect, to think about all of your blessings, to be thankful for what you have and what you have been given.

This year, as every year, I am thankful for friends and family. I am thankful for the time I get to spend with them. I am thankful my family is filled with very good cooks, who prepare an exquisite Thanksgiving feast for us to enjoy.

I am thankful for my two kittens who fill my home with laughter and light and love. I am thankful to have a new publishing business. I am thankful to have a job. I am thankful to have a car that can take me to my job. I am thankful I have a roof over my head.

I am thankful I have food to eat and diet soda to drink.

I am thankful to have a new computer.

I am thankful to have this blog for my means of expression.

I am thankful to you for reading my words on this blog.

I am thankful to have online friends from around the world.

I am thankful for everything I have been given, and everything I have not.

Sometime this holiday season, pause for a moment.

Think about all of your blessings, all you have been given, everything you are thankful for.

Give thanks.

A Union of Souls   December 4, 2013

A few days ago, a very good friend of mine gave birth to her
first child. A few years ago, she moved away. I have seen
photos from her life on social media, keeping in touch from a
far. I delighted in seeing photos from her wedding a couple
years ago. Over the last nine months, I had the pleasure of
seeing pictures she posted, watching her grow and glow in her
pregnancy. The baby was born in perfect health; mother and
baby were just fine. I was overjoyed at the news of the birth.
I was so happy for my friend and her husband.

Hearing the news of the birth of her child, I began to think
about the closest thing I have to children, my kittens.
Do not misunderstand me; I do not see my kittens as a
replacement for children, or to be the equivalent to a child.
They are my pets, and I love them. They share my home, and
have a place in my heart forever. But I do not consider them
my children.

My kittens, known in my writings as "Kit" and "Caboodle," are
15 months old now, and are no longer kittens officially (after
they are a year old, they are called cats.) However,
I love referring to them as my kittens. In terms of their
development, they are cats-teenagers to be exact. The days of
their thinking everything is a toy is long gone. Their favorite
toy is one another. They love to chase one another through the
house, wrestle and roughhouse together, and cuddle with one
another as they sleep.

I began to look at photos of them, and reflect on the time that
I adopted them from the shelter, just over a year ago.

I saw photos from their first night home, their first month, and their first year. The photos of the kittens are truly adorable. (What animal owner doesn't think their pets are adorable?)

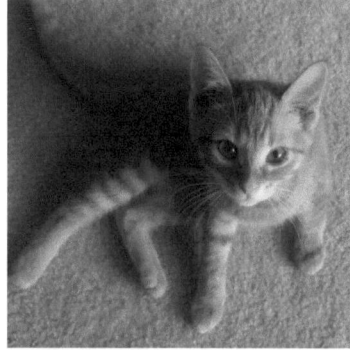

The kittens known as "Kit" and "Caboodle"

Seeing those photos, I remembered those first days, as the kittens got to know their new home, got to know me, and I got to know them. They are just like human beings; each animal has their own unique personality and temperament. One kitten loves to be held and cuddled; the other kitten likes affection when she likes it, on her terms.

I then thought about the love that we share, my love for the kittens, and their love for me. How did that happen? I knew I cared for the kittens the day I adopted them. I got to know their personalities, and within hours my caring turned to love. But, for the kittens, how did that happen? How did they come to love me? Do they love me because I am the only person they see and interact with? Or do they truly love me?

I think that, when you care for an animal, feed them, give them water, ensure their comforts, give them a safe, warm place for a home, they begin to trust you. That trust turns into love. Fifteen months later, the kittens come to me to be held and cuddled, and to share kitty kisses. I can say without a doubt that my kittens truly love me. And I truly love them. How does that bond happen? Does it appear from nothing? Did we create it? Were our souls meant to meet? The bond we feel with our pets, I feel, can only be understood and described as what it is- a union of souls.

Me holding "Kit" as she sleeps

Me rubbing "Caboodle's" back as she sleeps

26

Mandela   December 6, 2013

Yesterday the world lost a guiding light, a personal embodiment of forgiveness, tolerance, peace and hope. Nelson Mandela died at the age of 95 after a long struggle with a lung infection. He changed his country, the world forever. Rest in peace, Nelson "Madiba" Mandela.

*"Let us pause and give thanks
for the fact that Nelson Mandela lived—
a man who took history in his hands
and bent the arc of the moral universe
toward justice."
—President Barack Obama*

*"Today the world lost one of the true giants of the
past century. Nelson Mandela was a man
of incomparable honor, unconquerable strength,
and unyielding resolve—
a saint to many, a hero to all
who treasure liberty, freedom
and the dignity of humankind.
As we remember his triumphs,
let us, in his memory,
not just reflect on how far we've come,
but on how far we have to go.
Madiba may no longer be with us,
but his journey continues on with me
and with all of us."
-Morgan Freeman*

Thankful   December 7, 2013

Dear friends, I want to share a milestone with you. One year ago this month I launched this blog.

I began my first blog, Words of Hope, three years ago. I decided to change to a new blog, to take advantage of a new blog format, and the translation feature now available. It is important to me that people are able to read my writing in their own language.

To be honest, at first I was hesitant about moving to a new blog. I wondered if my readers would follow me. I worried about switching to a new page; yet, at the same time, I was excited about the new translation feature. I hoped that the change would make my work accessible to more readers.

To my delight, my hopes came true. In the past year, I have had over 14,800 visits to this blog, from readers in almost forty countries. On my first blog, I averaged about 100 visits a month. On this blog, I have averaged more than ten times that amount every month.

Here we are, one year later. So much has happened, so much has changed, and so much has stayed the same. I will write about the lessons I have learned from this year at another time. Yet I could not let this milestone go by without acknowledging it.

I have a grateful heart. I am truly thankful. I want to thank my friends and family, my online friends. From the bottom of my heart, I thank you. Your presence here means the world to me. Thank you for reading my words. Thank you for your support. Thank you for reading my letters to the moon.

Quiet Sunday   December 20, 2013

I awake to the sound of a meow. One of my cats is meowing to
the other. They notice I am awake. They meow at me to feed
them. I am home today. I do not have to work. I do not have to
go anywhere, see anyone. I do not feel well.

I am glad to be at home, especially because I do not feel well.
I lie motionless on the couch. I watch mindless television.
I love every second of it. Warm cozy blanket. One kitten lying
on my chest. The other kitten lies at my feet. They know I do
not feel well. They purr in contentment, glad to have me home,
all to themselves. Their presence helps me feel better.
Soft glow of the lights on the Christmas tree. So beautiful on
such an ugly, dark, grey winter day. I look out the window.
Snow flits through the sky. So peaceful and relaxing. So
beautiful with the lights of the Christmas tree, against a sky of
grey. Warm blanket. Cats to help me get well. Mindless
television to watch. Warm glow of Christmas lights and flitting
snow.

Relax. Breathe. Recuperate. Quiet Sunday.

"Grey Winter Day" by Esperanza Habla

The Path to Forgiveness   December 17, 2013

In the last year, I have begun to study and follow many life coaches and spiritual mentors. One of the mentors I follow is Iyanla Vanzant. She is a minister, spiritual leader, and a life coach. She has a weekly show on U.S. television; I find I learn something from every episode I watch.

Last week, Iyanla Vanzant posted on her Facebook page that she has a new book out on the topic of forgiveness. When I saw the post, I mentioned it to a friend who is going through a private, personal struggle, and is working on forgiveness.

Later that day I told another friend about the book, and that I hoped my library had ordered a copy of it. I would like to read it and learn more. This friend then asked me if I have forgiven the man who last broke my heart. My honest reply: "No, I have not."

I explained that, when it comes to forgiveness, I feel we have three choices:

*to forgive the person that wronged us
*to forgive the deeds the person did to us
*to do nothing and not forgive the person
or their deeds

I chose to forgive the deeds of the person, not the person themselves. The friend I was talking to paused a moment. She then asked me:
"What would it take for you to forgive him?"

My reply: "If he came to me and owned up to his behavior, if he was remorseful about what he had done, if he felt bad in his heart, if he truly apologized from his soul, I would forgive him."

My friend understood, yet she seemed disappointed by answer. She did not know how I could choose to forgive the deeds of the person, and not the person themselves. I then went on to clarify my answer....

"I cannot forgive that person without their being some remorse, and some form of an apology. The things he did were conscious, deliberate actions. He consciously chose those actions and behaviors."

My friend nodded her head in understanding. I then continued my thought....

"There is a path to forgiveness. Whether a person is forgiven, or their deeds, one of the most important parts of forgiveness is letting go. I had to learn that, even though I had done nothing wrong, I would not be getting an apology from the person who wronged me. I had to deal with that pain. I had to find a new normal, and to be okay in knowing the apology I deserve is never going to come. I had to know that within my soul and let it go. It is like the quote from Buddha about anger:
'Holding on to anger is like drinking poison and expecting the other person to die.'

Forgiveness is a very similar thing. If I do not forgive, then I am the one that suffers. I could not carry that hurt inside of me anymore. I had to work through the pain and let it go. In the time since the event happened, I have let go of it, and I have forgiven his deeds. That is all I can do."

The path to forgiveness is not an easy one. But it is truly a path, a process, a journey, one that requires caution and mindfulness with every step.

Holiday Moon
December 18, 2013

*a Letter to the Moon

Luna! So good to see you again! Thank you for visiting me a few weeks ago. I remember I had just gone to bed, and my bedroom was flooded with light. I instantly knew it was you. I looked out my window, and there you were. Thank you for coming to my bedroom window that night. It is so good to see you again. I have missed you the last few weeks. I saw you in the sky last night, almost full. It is so good to see your light in the dark winter sky.

How have you been? I have been fine. This is truly my favorite time of year, preparing for and enjoying the holidays. I love buying presents for my loved ones, and making my famous chocolate covered pretzels for friends and family to enjoy. I love to stay home, cuddle on the couch with my kittens, enjoy a cup of hot chocolate, and watch my favorite holiday movies.

The world is so beautiful during the holidays. Gorgeous snow-scapes in the forests, colorful window displays in the cities, fancily wrapped presents with bags and bows, angels and people made of snow, harmonious Christmas songs-both secular and scared-to sing along with, brightly colored Christmas lights that warm the chill of darkness of winter.

Do you have any plans for the holidays? Are you getting together with your brother the sun? I will be spending time with my family over the holidays. My family is so scattered, it seems the only time we can get together is in the holidays. But that just makes the time we do spend together that much sweeter. We gather as a family, go to church services on Christmas Eve, and share delicious holiday treats (like my chocolate covered pretzels!)

Unfortunately, madcap card games and football on television will make an appearance at the holidays.

But I will not let those spoil my holiday. Maybe we can squeeze in a trivia game, or a movie night. That would make the holiday fun.

I envy your vantage point; you can see all the beauty of the world has to offer during the holidays.

Yet, you can also see the pain and suffering, stress, depression and bitterness that sometimes accompany the holidays.

We often forget that the holidays are a time to gather together, to wish everyone love and light and peace on Earth.

Help us to remember this when we see your light.

Luna, my dear friend, I wish you a wondrous holiday season full of joy, love, light, laughter and peace.

Lessons from 2013   December 30, 3013

When I began to write three years ago, I began a journey of
self-examination and of self-discovery. It became important
for me to review the year I had experienced, reflect on what
had happened, what I had achieved, people I encountered,
challenges I overcame, how I had grown, the poems and pieces
I had written, and the lessons I had learned. I would now like
to share with you the lessons I have learned this year. Here
then are the lessons I have learned from 2013.

I have learned that...
> The world looks amazing, through my indigo colored
> glasses
> Ghosts from your past can only haunt you if you let
> them
> Going back to a story after a brief time away is like
> coming home, like visiting old friends
> I am grateful for what I have been given and what
> I have not
> Writing happens when inspiration comes
> Acts of kindness do not have to be random. In fact,
> they can be purposeful and deliberate
> Forgiveness is a conscious choice
> The moon is a beautiful gift to receive
> As I learn my craft, I improve my dedication
> It is a truly magical thing to have the moon smile
> at you
> Trust is like a crumpled up piece of paper. Once it has
> been crumpled up, it will never be the same again
> Adopting two loving kittens was one of the best things
> I ever did
> I am writing poems, expressing thoughts and opinions
> on this blog, and building a legacy
> I live a life of words
> This has been a powerful journey

Poetry is around us everywhere. Indeed, a divine
emollient

The pain of loss is thankfully temporary

I am writing poems, expressing thoughts and opinions
on this blog, and building a legacy

From time to time, we all need guidance

Being a writer gives me the power to create new
worlds, with infinite possibilities

The process of forgiveness is truly a journey of peace

Respect is given where respect is given

I am comforted to have the moon as my constant
guardian and friend

The writer's eye is equipped to discover many things

We are all citizens of the world

As I have grown as an artist, so has my confidence

Self-promotion is the name of the game

I feel that my writings are not poems, thoughts and
opinions, essays; I feel they are symphonies

Pray, listen, and be there for one another as life
altering changes occur

It was truly an honor for me to be chosen as the author
of the day

It is important to keep a promise once it is made, even
to the person who wronged you

As reading is indulgent to the reader, writing is as
indulgent to the writer

It is horrible to hear a chorus of noises when you
cannot sleep

Making charitable contributions to causes you believe
in is a wonderful way to pay it forward. The rewards
are innumerable

Being compared to a goddess is a wonderful thing,
especially a lunar goddess

If there is one thing this world needs on a global level,
and all of us need on an individual level, it is peace

Marriage equality is another step towards equality for
all

Although it was quite nerve wracking, I loved my first
photo shoot

I have stopped my quest, or pursuit of beauty. I no
longer need to seek what was within me all along.

Anyone can have misconceptions about anyone else,
for any reason

Justice is a term open to interpretation

The moon wears a mask. If you are lucky, she will let
you see the mask, as well as her true identity

What would this world be like without the four lads
from Liverpool?

I carry a grateful heart around with me every day

The meaning of life is...

The act of comparison is a waste of time and energy

Why did I not die in that swimming pool?

A writer works in silence, making the invisible visible

The internet is home to many things, including
friendship, love, sex, truth, lies, hope and hate

We are more alike than we are different

Fedoras can be lonely too

It is never easy, giving birth to a book

Love finds us when we least expect it

Scars heal, storms pass

I continue to work on tolerating the intolerant

I feel guided to help others as I have been helped

A life lived candidly is worthwhile indeed

In my thoughts and deeds I am a person of faith

No matter the letter or number on the label, the
clothes that fit your body and make you feel good about
yourself are the perfect fit

The nightmare continues

The life I desire is a life of abundance

Setbacks are normal occurrences in the path of life

Dreams do come true

I anxiously await the good things to come
I often receive my best, most fruitful ideas from the
    dream state
No matter the ways of celebrating, I feel that we
    should give thanks
The bond between a pet and their owner is truly
    a union of souls
I am sincerely thankful
Winter is truly an ugly and beautiful time, full of quiet
    Sundays
Do all that you can to complete the path to forgiveness
My favorite moon is the holiday moon

In looking back at these lessons, some came easily, some came
with difficulty. Some came from humor, some came through
pain. Yet, I am thankful for each and every lesson from this
year. I look forward to the lessons of the year to come.

I am thankful to you. With all of my heart, I wish you Happy
New Year, full of your own lessons.

> *"There is no wrong in being human.*
> *There are only lessons."*
> *-Iyanla Vanzant*

The Purging   January 4, 2014
(An internal monologue)

Day One
Finally, some time to work on things around the house.
I have so much to do. Where should I start? Maybe I will start
with this closet. I have to sort through everything in here. This
will take forever. I guess I should collapse down these
cardboard boxes first, to get them out of the way, and recycle
them later. Now, what to do with these things that are still in
here? Keep, donate to charity, or throw away. Those seem to
be my only options.

Wow, that did not take much time at all. Look at all this empty
space. What should I put in here? This might be a nice place to
put my Christmas decorations. I only need them once a year,
and they would be easy to get to here.

There, that looks great. Everything I wanted to keep fits in this
space. But now I have a closet in the other room that is half
empty. I wonder, could I clean that closet out as well? What all
do I have in there?

Day Three
I cannot believe that project on the closet took more than a
day. Well, it is a walk-in closet, about three times the size of
my other closets. But, today is a new day. I should get to work
on these bags full of paper. I have to sort through all of this, to
see what if anything is garbage, what I have to keep, and what
I should put through a shredder for security purposes.

I cannot believe it has been three hours already; I'm only
about hallway through these papers. But I cannot quit.
I have to get this done today. I am determined.

Hey, what is this? I do not believe it. It is my last letter to the Little Prince. Oh and here is his reply to me. Why do I have this? Why did I save this? I need to shred this. The conversation did not mean anything then, it does not mean anything now. I need to shred these papers, delete this from my memory bank, and move on.

Day Five

Wow, the house looks great. I cannot believe I started this project five days ago. I did not mean to work on that many projects around the house. But, when I accomplished one task, it inadvertently lead into another. Now that it is all done, I have boxes full of things to donate to charity, and bags of shredded paper and cardboard to recycle.

It looks amazing in here. I literally have half of the material possessions that I did a week ago. I feel that a massive weight has been lifted. I feel lighter. I feel a sense of order, clarity, calm, and peace. I should have done this purging months ago.

"Peace cannot exist in disorder.
When things are out of order,
there will be chaos and confusion.
When there is chaos and confusion,
things cannot be clear.
When you are clear, you are peaceful."
-Iyanla Vanzant

Ion   January 11, 2014

Last week, the U.S. experienced two winter storms. The first storm laid 6 inches of snow locally. Three days later, there was another storm-a behemoth storm, unlike any other. Its name was Ion. "A thirty year storm" they called it. The storm was said to have been reminiscent of a blizzard that happened in 1978. I remember that blizzard.

I remember sitting in our living room; our windows, which went from the floor to ceiling, were entirely covered with snow. Winter storm Ion brought almost 12 inches of snow, which was, ironically, more snow than we received in the blizzard of 1978.

The Polar Vortex was the second part of the storm, the deadliest part of the storm. An area of cold air normally located at the North Pole and South Poles, the Polar Vortex visited half of the United States. It was colder in parts of the U.S. than at either of the poles.

The temperature in the wind reached -50 degrees below zero (Fahrenheit) in my town. News reports said a person could be dead within minutes without the proper attire. The whole of the United States did not have the proper attire for those temperatures.

The winter storm was deadly. More than 20 people across the United States died. People outside shoveling the snow collapsed from having a heart attack, from the strain it caused to their heart. People and animals that were caught outside perished from exposure to the cold. Trees laden with ice and snow fell to the ground, often taking nearby power lines down with them.

Thousands were stuck in their homes without heat or electrical power. Buildings collapsed from the buildup of ice and snow. Those that were blessed with power consumed more energy in those four days than most communities use in an entire year. During the storm, and for days after, motorists were met with compacted snow that turned into sheets of ice that were inches thick. Cars became hockey pucks on the snow and ice, being tossed and bumped in every direction.

My interaction with Ion was thankfully limited. I was stuck in my home for four days, during the snowstorm and in its aftermath. My friends and family were safe at home, out of the winter chill. My car was parked outside on the day of the storm. In the days after the storm, I had to dig my car out from an igloo of snow; it took me four hours over the course of two days.

© *Esperanza Habla*

The Dream State

When I ventured out of my neighborhood, the streets were not safe for travel. To say the roads were hazardous would be an understatement. Thankfully I made it to my workplace, and back home that night, safe and sound. I prayed to every deity to get me-and my car-home in one piece.

A week later, the winds have changed. The Polar Vortex has gone back to the poles, taking its dangerous conditions with it. The temperatures are above the freezing mark. Mother Nature cleared the streets before the city could. Roads are drivable again. So far this season, my state has received more snow than we see in an entire year. The 18 inches of snow is beginning to melt. The precipitation now falls as rain. The dangerous weather is over, for now.

The day the storm raged I took photographs of the snowfall in the trees.....

© *Esperanza Habla*

© *Esperanza Habla*

Nature can be dangerously beautiful.

Goodbye winter storm Ion. Goodbye Polar Vortex. I hope it takes another thirty years to have a similar thirty-year snowstorm.

If you were to ask me, "How do you feel now that the Polar Vortex and winter storm Ion have gone away?"

My answer to that question is a one word answer.

Happy.

A Letter on HJR3   January 23, 2014

In my state of Indiana the issue of marriage equality is up for a vote. Lawmakers are trying to pass a bill labeled HJR3, which would permanently change our state constitution to define marriage as between one woman and one man only. I have written a letter to Indiana lawmakers about my views on marriage equality and equal rights for all. Here then is my letter, "A Letter on HJR3".....

To whom it may concern:

I am writing to you about the HJR3 proposed amendment to the Indiana state constitution which defines marriage as between one man and one woman.

Let me first start by saying that I am a Christian, I am single and I am heterosexual. I was not born in Indiana, but have lived here for 41 years. Indiana is my home.

I understand that many have strong views on homosexuality, some of which are religion based, while others are based in fear. If you are opposed to same sex marriage, I hope you will open your heart and mind to listen to what I have to say.

It must be understood that the issue of marriage equality has nothing to do with religion. The separation of church and state should guarantee this truth. Marriage equality is not a religious issue, but one of civil rights. The people of this state deserve to have their civil rights preserved, regardless of who they love.

Hoosiers should have the right to marry the person they love. As I am single, I have not yet met the man I am to marry. When that time comes, I would not want anyone to go into a voting booth and vote on my right to marry the man I love. Likewise, I should not be afforded rights that are denied others just because I was born heterosexual.

In the Preamble to the U.S. Constitution, it gives all Americans the inalienable rights to "life, liberty, and the pursuit of happiness." In the Declaration of Independence, Thomas Jefferson wrote that "all men are created equal." Article 1 of the Universal Declaration of Human Rights states that:

"All human beings are born free and equal in dignity and rights. They are endowed with reason and conscience and should act towards one another in a spirit of brotherhood."

Marriage equality is not an issue of religion. It is an issue of rights. Basic, human, inalienable, equal, civil rights. Period. End of sentence.

Do not let this issue go to the voters in November. Reject this proposed amendment to the Indiana constitution.
Thank you.

"But here's the thing about equal rights-
they're not actually supposed to be voted on.
That's why they're called rights."
-Rachel Maddow

A Lesson in Patience   January 28, 2014

It is not always easy, to be a writer. It is often difficult to get the stars to align and for the thoughts to come out.

I put the thoughts on paper. I read what I have written. Does any of it make sense? Is any of it worth sharing?

Sometimes the muse Calliope, the muse of poetry, comes, and creativity abounds. The stars align; the words come together and flow out of me like a waterfall.

Yet other times my muse is elusive. Inspiration hides from me. In those moments, I feel like the myth of Sisyphus, confined to a fate of rolling a massive bolder up a hill, only to have it come hurdling towards the Earth again. The words remain stuck. The stars do not align.

In these moments I have learned not to press the issue. I have learned that Calliope will come, the stars will align, and the words will flow. I must give it time. I must be patient with myself. I must be patient and wait for my muse to arrive, to wait for the stars to align.

It can be an act of futility, and undoubtedly a lesson in patience.

The Creation of Art   February 6, 2014

I am currently working on the finishing touches, the last few details, on my first book of poetry. The book is called "I am Hope", a collection of my first poems, many of which never made it to either of my blogs. I am in the last stages of getting the book ready for publication. After "I am Hope" is published, I will publish a book of the same poetry in Spanish. My second book, "the Bigger Picture", will be the next to be released. It too will have a Spanish version. The books will be available in print and in electronic versions.

When I set out to create my own publishing company, I originally thought that I would publish all of my books of poetry at the same time. To have two books come out in English and in Spanish-in both print and electronic versions-at the same time would have been a monumental effort. It is stressful enough publishing one book! Now that I know all that goes into the making of a book, I will never look at a book the same way again.

There are so many things to check, double check, make sure that everything is exactly as you want it. If you change one thing, it invariably changes another thing, and then another, and so on. This rippling effect is hard to avoid and hard to control. Once you feel you have everything organized and in check, things spiral out of control. It feels as hopeless as trying to herd a bunch of cats.

Now that I am working on the finishing touches on the book, I feel that I have everything in check, and that publication is imminent. Watch this space.

It is said that the creation of art, creating something from nothing, is much like the birthing process. The process takes time, and cannot be rushed. The art will be created when it is meant to be.

The next time you see a painting, a sculpture, watch a movie, hear a symphony, read a book, I urge you to pause for just a moment. Take time to examine that piece of art. Try to imagine everything it took to bring that creation of art to reality.

Hello Luna

February 23, 2014

(a Letter to the Moon)

Hello Luna, my dear friend. How are you? How have you
been? Thank you for stopping by the other night for a visit.
I am sorry that I was not able to visit with you that night.
I am sorry that I have not written in a while, and have been
"radio silent" recently. I have not been well at all. The start of
2014 has been challenging for me, in terms of my health.
I have been sick for weeks.

Everything began about a month ago, when I went to get an
inoculation for influenza. I knew I should have gotten the shot
earlier in winter; however I was confident that I would still be
protected from the flu virus. When I got the flu shot, the
doctor said it would take 2 weeks before the shot would take
effect. I did not know that until he said it. Still, I had a sense of
security, knowing I was doing the right thing, getting the flu
shot at all. It proved to be a false sense of security. Two weeks
later-to the day-I became ill, with a cold.

When I had the first inkling that I was getting sick,
I rebelled. I thought, "No, I do not have time to be sick!
I cannot be sick! I have to work! I cannot be sick!" All of this
rebellion was for naught. I had to face reality, no longer deny
the inevitable, and surrender to the virus.

The cold lasted for two weeks. I was not miserable, but
uncomfortable to be sure. I found two weeks to be an
inordinately long amount of time to be sick. Eventually the
virus left me. After the cold was over, it was more than a week
before I began to feel normal. However, normal would not last.

About a week ago, I went to bed feeling different. Something
was off, yet I did not know what. I would shortly find out.

The Dream State

I woke up 5 hours later with digestive problems. This time, when the illness struck, I had no time to rebel. I was instantly sick. The virus came and hit me like a truck. A day into the illness I went to the doctor. After an examination, the doctor found that I had a live virus in my intestines. She said that this was an airborne virus that was going around, and that the recovery time would be painfully slow. She gave me a prescription for some medicine, and some guidelines on what to do in the coming days to get better faster.

I recovered at home for a week. I could not go to work because I was contagious, and had a myriad of problems. I was constantly nauseated for three days. I had a constant migraine headache which lasted for two days. All of the nausea and headache issues were in addition to the digestion issues I was experiencing. When you came to visit me Luna, I was so ill. I remember lying in bed, and noticing the room flood with your light. I lifted my head and looked out the window. There you were, shining in all of your glory. I remember saying hello to you, and laying my head down again. I wanted to talk to you, to have a proper visit with you. But, I simply could not. However, I am so glad you came. I felt so comforted, knowing you were there, watching over me as I slept.

A week has passed since I fell ill. I am slowly adding more food selections to my limited menu, to train my stomach to accept food again. There is a saying Luna, maybe you have heard it- "You did not know what you had until it was gone." I feel that way, about my health. There have only been 8, 9 weeks in this New Year, and I have been sick for 3 of them! In the coming months, I will be more mindful about my health and what foods I put into my body. I tell you Luna, I have had enough health issues this year. I am ready to focus on other things-like publishing my book! These issues with my health have been a setback in that goal, to be sure.

Before I leave you, I want to show you something. I have been looking for a graphic artist for months to help me design a logo for my publishing company, La Luna Press.

I finally found a great artist named Adam Whitaker. He worked on the design, and I offered my input. Adam came up with an amazing image to represent my company.
I think you will love it. I'm honored to show you the design. Here it is....

Designed by Adam Whitaker: www.adamwhitaker.com

I love the design. I love how you are represented.

I absolutely love the logo. I could not have asked for anything else.

The stars are aligning, Luna. Everything will come together soon. I will let you know as soon as the book is ready.

Take care Luna. Talk to you soon.

A Card for my Mom February 27, 2014

Cancer. It can be a terrifying word. I know I was terrified when my mother told me that she had cancer. I remember being caught up in the word-"cancer." I did not know my mother's condition, that there were 4 stages of cancer, which stage my mother was in, what her course of treatment would be, or anything else. The first word that people think of when they hear the word cancer is "death." At least that was the first word I thought of. Up to that point in my life, my brief history with cancer was death. Three friends of mine had cancer and did not survive.

When my friends battled their cancers, I sent them greeting cards, to let them know I was thinking of them. "Why send them a greeting card?" you might ask. Quite simply, it was the only thing I knew to do. I felt helpless. I could not control the situation, the progression of the disease, or what was happening. The only thing I could do for them was to send a greeting card to express my concern, encouragement, and well wishes. When my mother went through her cancer treatment, I sent her greeting cards as well. I sent her a greeting card a week, sometimes more often than that. At the end of her treatment, she had an abundance of cards and letters and well wishes from friends and family.

Thankfully, my mother's cancer was treatable. She received a course of treatment customized for her, and made a full recovery. She was diagnosed with cancer ten years ago today. She remains cancer free to this day.

Congratulations mom on your surviving ten years cancer free. I hope you like this card. I made it just for you.

Art for Art's Sake   March 11, 2014

I read an article the other day that greatly disturbed me; it was an article about a man being executed.

His government accused him of many things, yet the definition of his guilt is open to interpretation. The crime he was put to death for-being a poet. When I first saw this story I could not fathom it. A man was killed for being a poet. He was hanged for creating art, expressing himself, voicing his views and opinions. I remember staring at the computer screen. The information would not absorb into my brain. I am an American-freedom of speech is a right that we hold dear. Yet this right is not exclusive to the U.S. This right is found in the Universal Declaration of Human Rights, and recognized as law in the International Covenant on Civil and Political Rights. I am sure that the execution of this poet is not the first "punishment" of its kind. I wonder if his execution is in violation of this very law. Hearing this story made me think about my life as an artist, my work. I am grateful that I have found a new voice in my writing. I am grateful I have writing as a means to express myself. I cannot imagine having my art used as evidence against me, proof enough to sign my death sentence. My thoughts turn to other poets, filmmakers, songwriters, comedians, musicians and other artists who express themselves through art. How different this world would be without opinion or satire, social or political commentary.

Is art a means of expression or an act of treason? Are you an artist? Would you be willing to die for the right to express your art?

Gifts   March 20, 2014

All of us have been given gifts in our life. Whether your gift is cooking a delicious meal, painting a portrait, writing a song, working with animals, making a movie, working with children, we all have our own, individual, unique gifts.

I believe they were picked just for us, and given to us for a reason. When I grew up, I was classically trained as a singer. I sang in choirs in churches and schools, and studied privately, for twenty-five years. I knew my singing voice was a gift. I felt my purpose on this planet was to be a singer. However, after a tonsillectomy, my voice, or what my voice had been, was taken from me. I felt I had lost my gift. However, through my writing, I have discovered my true gift. I was not put on this Earth to be a singer; I was put on this planet to use my voice. Whether through song or writing, I feel my voice is my gift. I have often thought of my gift of writing, and my life as an artist. I find that, after my evening prayers, I get most of my inspiration in the dream state.

That makes me wonder-does my writing come from me? Am I being guided in my writing? Am I being given inspiration as well? I know that I have been surprised at some of the things I have written. In looking back at my earliest work, I thought: "I wrote that?" I know that much of my inspiration comes from daily life. I feel I have been given a writer's eye to help me find inspiration and interpret the information. However, I have felt that I am being guided on my journey, and that the inspiration I receive is indeed a gift. In my life as an artist, I have met artists of other fields from around the globe. One such artist described himself not as an artist, or performer, but as a vessel. He recognized that his talent was his gift, and felt he could not take credit for his work, because God was working through him.

Is that true for all of us, in all of our gifts? Does God work through me in my writing? Is my writing mine, or divine?

I do feel guided as an artist. I feel that someone-or something-plants a seed of a thought in my brain, and I am the one that is responsible for its cultivation.

We are all uniquely different and the same. We were given our gifts for a reason, and it is up to us to act on them.

As for me, I am a willing instrument for the gods and goddesses I serve. I am open to positive, divine inspiration to come my way. I will interpret it, write my truth, what I see through my writer's eye.

That is my purpose and my gift. Now that I have found my gift, I intend to play on, learn my craft, and become a skilled instrument.

Sunflowers   March 30, 2014

Hello Sally, my dear friend. How are you? I trust our friend Luna is keeping you well.

I had to write to you today. You left us three years ago today. I remember it as if it happened last week.

I have thought about you a lot in the last few weeks. One of the ladies we worked with in the library will soon be on her journey to heaven, will soon begin her metamorphosis into radiant light.

It made me think of you, the letters I sent you, the cards I sent you, during your illness, leading up to your metamorphosis into light.

I want to send our friend a letter, to let her know she is in my thoughts. However, she and I are not close like you and I were. I found myself asking my friends and family what to write her.

What do you say, what do you write in your last letter to someone?

I think I have found something to write her about. Someone recently asked about her in the library. I think I will share that story with her. I know it will cheer her. I have really missed you Sally. I am sorry you lost your battle with cancer, and had to leave us.

But, I know you are in heaven with the Lord. I am sure that is where you want to be. I remember recently hearing some exciting news. My first thought was, "I cannot wait to tell Sally." Then I remembered. I do not have to tell you. You already know.

My mind goes to the song I used to send you. It always makes me think of you. It awakens memories of you, conversations we had together, going to your visitation, the numerous photos I saw from your life, seeing you in your casket, adorned with sunflowers.

Thank you for coming into my life, for your friendship, and for everything you have taught me. Thank you for the sunflowers.

Filters   April 9, 2014

One of the things I love to do in my free time, apart from writing, is taking photographs. I am not a professional photographer, by any means. Still, I love capturing a moment in time. I love taking photos of things of beauty...

...a new fallen snow....

Snow with black and white filter
© Esperanza Habla

...a pretty flower...

Orchid with a color filter
© Esperanza Habla

...fun special effects...

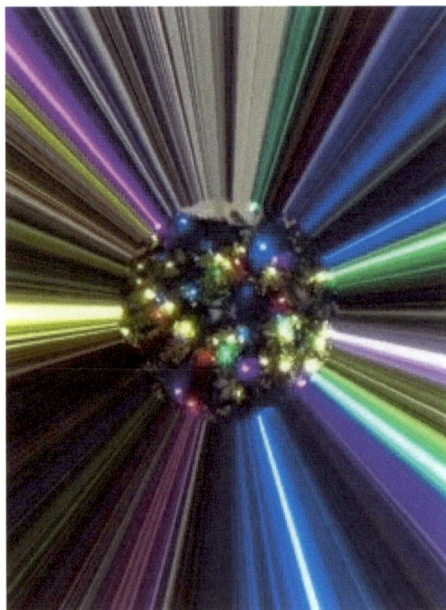

My Christmas tree, with a kaleidoscope filter
© Esperanza Habla

...my friend Luna, the moon, in all her glory.

© *Esperanza Habla*

Along with taking photographs digitally, I love to edit them. I own a tablet, and have access to several programs, or applications, to help me edit my photos. Sometimes the picture I took was too dark, too light, had too much color, not enough color, or did not turn out the way I wanted it to. Editing the photo through the use of different effects, or "filters", enables me to enhance the photo, to capture the moment I wanted to share.

The wonders of digital photography and editing programs means that an image can be manipulated as little, or as much as the viewer wants. Take for example my logo for my publishing company, La Luna Press, designed by my friend Adam Whitaker...

And here is my logo, again, but edited with a digital filter....

While playing with the different filters in the photography program, I began to notice that while I was enhancing the photo, I was also making it something different altogether. The original photo is wonderful, as is the variation. But is it necessary?

Going through this process in editing photos, it made me think about how we do this in our daily lives. We all use filters. What we see is defined by our view on the world. We edit what we see before us. Our perceptions of ourselves, the world around us, is all filtered. Our eyes act as both the camera and the filter. As a result, we find things we did not see before, put things in a better light, miss things we should have seen.

Maybe we should look at the world as a photographer would, looking through the viewfinder on her camera when getting ready to take a photograph. Maybe we should look at things from a new perspective. Maybe we should take a step back, pause a moment, and look at the bigger picture.

Perhaps the view in front of us is perfect as it is. Perhaps the photograph does not need a filter after all.

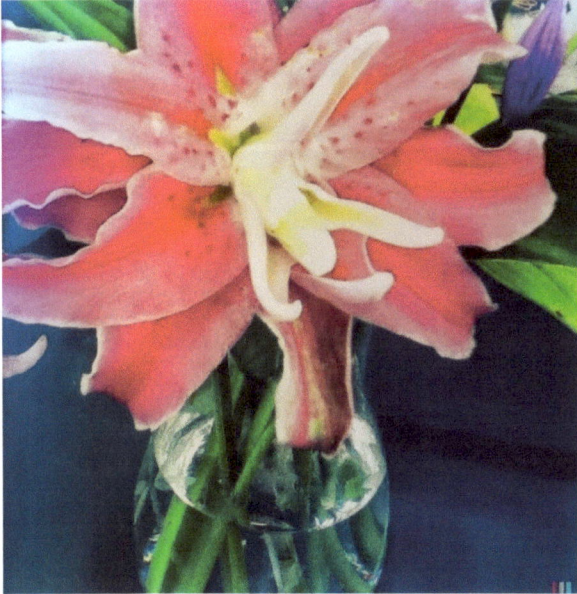

Same orchid as shown before, no filters
© Esperanza Habla

The Dream State

Birthday Moon   April 17, 2014
*A letter to the moon

Hello Luna my dear friend. Thank you so much for coming to visit me on my birthday. It was sweet of you to come.

I saw on the news that you had an eclipse the other day. That is right, you made the news! Unfortunately there was an abundance of clouds that night and I was unable to witness the eclipse myself. I saw some photos of your lunar event. In fact, one of my online friends took some photos of you. You looked truly breathtaking. I was elated to see you the next night, shining in all of your glory. I was able to take some photos of you that night. I even captured your mask again. I hope you like them...

© Esperanza Habla

© *Esperanza Habla*

I remember seeing you that night; I can see you in my mind's eye.

I wonder, Luna, if you know the comfort your light brings. When I look at you, I am home.

It was so good to see you Luna.

Thank you for coming, for illuminating the midnight sky.

What a truly wondrous gift-a birthday moon.

The Discovery April 27, 2014

It is a terrifying thing, when you are told that something might be medically wrong with you. Such a thing happened to me last week. I was home on a vacation from work. I did not travel; instead I did errands in town and chores in and around my house. One of the tasks I had to complete was an eye examination with my eye doctor. I go once a year to get my eyes tested, have an eye examination, and usually get fitted for new glasses. It is always a routine examination. However, this last visit was anything but routine. The examination begins with tests for the eye, with various tests.

> **"Look through here; focus your eye here;
> hold your head this way; open your eyes wide;
> do not blink."**

One of the machines was new this year-a machine to examine the internal workings of the eye, including the retina. This is where things became scary.

My eye doctor examined my eyes, and then looked at the results of the tests I had just completed. It was then that the doctor discovered an area of pigmentation on my retina. She then said that this was the reason I have been having so many headaches. I have had occasional headaches for years. As my eyesight has changed, my headaches have increased, and I began to have migraine headaches. A migraine is a type of headache that has severe symptoms. Some of the symptoms of a migraine include significant pain in the head, sensitivity to light, sensitivity to sound, nausea, and even temporary changes in personality-all of which I have experienced in the past.

I have always had a feeling that my eyes were the reason
I was having headaches. This simple scan from this new piece
of equipment answered many questions. Yet, at the same time,
it generated many new ones.

After pointing out the area of pigmentation on my retina, my
doctor said we would have to monitor the situation closely.
I asked her why it needed to be monitored so closely; her
response was because the area of pigmentation is so close to
my brain.

That statement terrified me. I could see the doctor was
concerned, and now, so was I. I left the appointment feeling
nervous about what the doctor had said. Her words echoed
through my brain. I could not get her words out of my mind.

The next day, I went to a medical website online to learn about
pigmentation of the retina and what it meant. I searched and
was then taken to a page that briefly described it. The page
also listed symptoms and scenarios that accompany this
discovery-symptoms and scenarios that may one day be my
reality.

The first example was pigmentation on the retina with
headaches. The second scenario was with headaches and
migraines. Another scenario showed pigmentation with tunnel
vision. The last scenario was complete blindness.

It is ironic that, with this new diagnosis, one that is changing
my vision, is increasing my sight. I already see the world
around me quite differently. It is as if I am learning to see
again-or learning to stop and take notice of what I see. It has
also increased my desire to travel, to see more of this beautiful
world, before the opportunity is taken away from me.

The Dream State

As scary as this discovery is, I am grateful to know about the pigmentation on my retina so my doctor can cautiously monitor it. If the medical office had not gotten this new piece of equipment, I still would not know the cause of my headaches.

No one knows what the future will bring. I do not know that this pigmentation will rob me of my sight; however, I do not know that it will not.

This discovery has been an awakening, has made me open my eyes, to take notice of the world around me. It has made me take notice of myself, in my body. I need to be observant and mindful to how I am feeling.

If I have the slightest twinge of a headache, I need to take medicine so that it will not progress and become a migraine. If I happen to have a migraine that comes out of nowhere, which I have experienced many times, I need to take medicine for it and ride the wave until it is gone.

This discovery has been terrifying for me. I am scared about what the future could possibly bring.

This discovery is a call to action, to be mindful and observant, to be careful, cautious and proactive.

This might be the worst thing that could ever happen to me. Or it might be the best. It remains to be seen.

"I am learning to see.
I don't know why it is,
but everything enters me more deeply
and doesn't stop where it once used to."
-Rainer Marina Rilke

Life, Death, Art, Immortality   May 14, 2014

There was a sad turn of events recently; a family member died. I was not close to this family member, but the loss was felt by all. I traveled with members of my family for the funeral services.

In times like these, it is natural to think about our own mortality. At one point my family members asked me if I have made plans for my demise. Yes, I have made plans.

I would like to be cremated, and have my ashes scattered in a beautiful place. I have not decided where yet. Maybe Paris. That way, if I never get to Paris, I will one day.

With all this talk and contemplation on death, I am reminded of something one of my online friends, an actor, told me once. He said that artists never die. Our work lives on long after we do. Through our work, we attain immortality.

To be truthful, I had never thought about it that way before. But yet I can see that it is true. With the examples of the films of Charlie Chaplin, the songs of John Lennon, the books of Maurice Sendak, the paintings of Van Gogh, art lives on.

I am not a writer, an artist, to achieve immortality. But I realize that, in my writings here, and when I publish my books of poetry, my words will live on forever. As long as the written word is relevant to human kind, I will survive.

I think back to the visitation for my family member. The room was filled with family. I wondered who will still be around when my time comes to go to heaven.

The Dream State

I do not have a big family. I am not married. I have no children. I have nieces and nephews. There will probably not be a big gathering. I may not even have a visitation. Maybe a party instead.

Although it may not be a big event, I do not really need one. I do not need a room full of people to remember me. Eventually, those people will be gone themselves. Memories of me, of them, will be gone forever.

I did not realize when I became a writer that I would achieve immortality. However, I am comforted by it. I consider myself lucky and honored to have this gift.

When it is my time to go, I will know that I will live on through my words. I will know that I have been loved.

Yet Again   May 18, 2014

Life is full of meetings and partings, hellos and goodbyes, arrivals and farewells, love and loss. Each day comes with its own challenges.

Some days the severity of a loss does not affect you, and you can ride the wave. Other times the wave crashes on top of you without warning, leaving you breathless in its wake.

There have been many challenges for me this year, this month. I recently shared that one of my family members has died. Yet again there has been another loss in my life. This time I have lost a dear friend.

One of my former co-workers at the library died a few days ago. She and I were friends while we worked together; when she retired, she and I drifted apart.

We would send one another e-mail messages occasionally, usually on holidays. Even though we did not interact as often as we had in the past, we picked up our friendship just where we left off.

I learned that this friend had cancer a couple of months ago. A few weeks ago she entered hospice, or end of life care.

I was told by her family that cards and letters were welcomed. Upon hearing that, I decided to write my dying friend a letter.

However, that brought me much pause. What do you write when you know it will be the very last time you will communicate with that person? What do you write in the last letter you will ever send to a friend?

The Dream State

After a few days of thinking, I decided on what to send her.
I sent her a greeting card and wrote a special message inside.

I then enclosed one of the poems I have written, "It's Quiet in
the Library Today." When I wrote it, I wrote about having an
unusually quiet day in the library. Now the library is quiet for
another reason-to honor her memory.

Now that my friend has died it brings me solace to know that
she is in heaven, and she is no longer in pain.

Her loss is already felt by those that loved her.

There is one more star in the sky.

Rest in peace, dear friend.

About the Author

Esperanza Habla is the pen name of the Indigo Poet of the Moon. She began her writing career in 2010. She has had two blogs to date, "Words of Hope" and "Letters to the Moon", which has garnered a readership in more than 80 countries worldwide.

In 2013 she formed her own publishing company, La Luna Press, L.L.C. Esperanza's first book of poetry, "I am Hope", was published in April of 2015.

Esperanza holds a degree in Music History and Literature from Marian University. Esperanza has been featured in the Poetry Daily and received nominations for an Indiana Authors Award in 2015 and 2016.

To date she had published four books in English and two in Spanish.

www.lalunapress.com
www.esperanzahabla.com

Other publications from La Luna Press:

I am Hope

The first poetic
collection by
Esperanza Habla

Soy Esperanza

El primer
colección poética
por
Esperanza Habla

The Bigger Picture

The second
poetic collection
by Esperanza Habla

El Panorama

El segundo
colección poética
por
Esperanza Habla

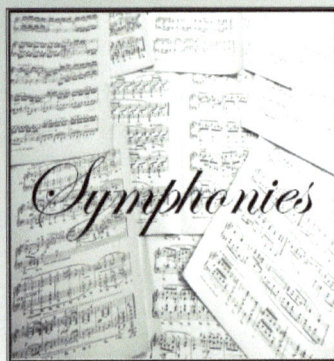

Symphonies

The third poetic collection
by
Esperanza Habla